MW01611514

# Animals

by James Metzger

 **HOUGHTON MIFFLIN HARCOURT**
School Publishers

PHOTOGRAPHY CREDITS: Cover © Jeffrey Jackson/Alamy; 1 © Mike Hutchings/Reuters/Corbis; 3 (tl) © Peter Adams/JAI/Corbis, (tr) © Getty, (m) © Corbis, (b) © Corbis; 5 (tl) © Ken Welsh/Age Foto Stock, (tr) © PhotoDisc, (bl) © Russell Illig/Age Foto Stock, (br) © Kevin Schafer/Alamy; 7 (tl) © Pixland/Corbis, (tr) © Paul A. Souders/Corbis, (m) © Caetano Barreira/Epa/Corbis, (b) © Mike Hutchings/Reuters/Corbis; 9 (tl) © Dinodia Photo Library/Brand X, (tr) © Tony Wharton; Frank Lane Picture Agency/Corbis, (bl) © Tony Wharton; Frank Lane Picture Agency/Corbis, (br) © Jeffrey Jackson/Alamy; 10 (tl) © Getty Images, (tr) © Getty Images/Rubberball, (bl) © Paul Edmondson/Corbis

Printed in China

ISBN-13: 978-0-547-42735-5
ISBN-10: 0-547-42735-2

2 3 4 5 6 7 8 0940 18 17 16 15 14 13 12 11 10

This animal lives in
a cold place.
It has white fur
and sharp claws.
It uses ==those== claws
to hunt.
It is a bear!

This animal lives in a hot place.
It has green feathers and a beak.
It can **fly** **or** it can **walk**.
It is a **bird**!

This animal lives
in the water.
It lives in ==both== hot
and cold places.
It has a big mouth
and a ==long== tail.
It is a whale!

This animal lives in the forest.
It has big ears
and very small ==eyes==.
It has a long trunk.
It is an elephant!

This animal lives in a house.
It has strong arms and white teeth.
What is it?

# Responding

**Word Builder**

Birds can fly.  What other animals can fly?

**Talk About It**

**Text to World** Draw a picture of a bird.  Share the picture with your class.  Tell about the bird.

| | |
|---|---|
| **bird** | **long** |
| **both** | **or** |
| **eyes** | **those** |
| **fly** | **walk** |

**TARGET STRATEGY** **Monitor/Clarify**

Find ways to figure out what doesn't make sense.